UNOFFICIAL

Bridgerton
Embroidery

20 Patterns Inspired by the
World of Regency Romance

Hilary LESLIE

Contents

4 Welcome, Dearest Gentle Stitchers

7   TOOLS & MATERIALS
8   BASIC TECHNIQUES
10 COMMON STITCHES
17 FINISHING YOUR WORK
17 DISPLAYING YOUR EMBROIDERIES

18 The Ton's First Stitches
  20 Penelope's Blossoms
  24 A Posy of Violets
  28 The Duke's Rose Garden
  32 Wisteria on the Promenade
  36 A Scandalous Quill
  40 The Secret Hive
  44 Featherington's Flowers
  48 The Gentleman's Balloon
  52 Music in the Drawing Room
  56 A Cake Fit for a Duchess

60 Fit for the Queen
  62 Unwed Monogram
  66 The Residence
  70 Garden Swing Whispers
  74 Danbury's Diadem
  78 Tea with the Ton
  82 The Regency Teacup
  86 Mystery of the Masquerade
  90 Butterflies and Bubbly
  94 The Blooming Bee
  98 Your Carriage Awaits

102 TEMPLATES
110 ABOUT THE AUTHOR
111 INDEX
112 ACKNOWLEDGMENTS

Welcome, Dearest Gentle Stitchers

If you're spellbound by the romance and beauty of the Regency era, you've come to the right place!

For centuries, needlework was a popular pastime for women and girls. Embroidery could be found in a wide variety of places, including samplers and linens, royal wear, and ecclesiastical decor. Embroidered pieces were not limited to just needle and thread. Some historic pieces feature beads, sequins, and metallic threads.

If you've picked this book up because you've read or watched the *Bridgerton* series, you may have noticed embroidery hoops in the hands of the leading ladies. As they share gossip about the latest romances, they pass their needles through the fabric the same way we do today.

The hit Netflix series brought the characters from Julia Quinn's books to life in such a visually spectacular way, I couldn't help but be inspired. Using themes, motifs, and colors from the Regency era and the *Bridgerton* world, I've designed twenty hoops to show your love of the craft and the period.

If you're new to embroidery, read through the sections on basic techniques and common stitches. I've provided you step-by-step guidance so you'll be successful with your first project. The designs featured in "The Ton's First Stitches" are very beginner friendly; I suggest starting there. If you're a seasoned stitcher, you'll enjoy the ease of those projects as well, or you can jump right into the more advanced projects in "Fit for the Queen."

Now is the perfect time to queue up your favorite episode, pour a cup of tea, grab your needle and thread, and get lost in a time gone by.

Happy stitching,

Hilary

Tools & Materials

First things first, you'll need the right tools to get started on your embroidery journey. You can find these supplies at your local craft store, or you can order them online.

EMBROIDERY FLOSS

Embroidery floss is what will make your design come to life, and it is available in a myriad of beautiful colors! DMC is my preferred brand to use and is very popular amongst embroidery artists. DMC floss is made up of six individual strands. Using more strands creates a fuller, chunkier look, while fewer strands are great for fine detail work or thread painting. Match the color code on the floss label to the number provided in the pattern to recreate the exact look shown.

TIP: *Always pull your floss from the bottom of the skein (the end with the barcode and color code) to avoid tangling!*

HOOPS

Embroidery hoops are what hold your fabric in place while you're stitching. They're available in a variety of sizes, measured based on their diameter from edge to edge. I prefer to work with bamboo hoops most of the time. I also love the faux wood options made by Anchor.

NEEDLES

There are many needle varieties you can use for embroidery depending on your project and comfort level! The eye of the needle—the opening where you thread your floss—comes in many sizes. Embroidery needles have a smaller eye, while tapestry and chenille needles have a larger eye, which are great for projects using all six strands of floss or thicker embroidery threads, such as tapestry wool.

Needle sizes vary as well: Some are longer and thinner, while others are shorter and thicker. Don't be afraid to experiment with different kinds!

TIP: *Keep in mind that if you have a tighter weave of fabric, thicker needles such as tapestry and chenille will leave behind larger holes in your fabric as you're stitching.*

SCISSORS

You'll need scissors not only for cutting your embroidery floss throughout the stitching process but to prep your fabric as well. Fabric scissors are very handy to have for cutting your fabric of choice with crisp lines.

FABRIC

Fabric choice often comes down to personal preference, but you should be sure to buy cloth that doesn't stretch. Linen, my favorite to work with, is a popular choice, as is cotton. Don't be afraid to experiment with different colored fabrics too! Colored fabric can make a fun, bold contrast to your stitching, depending on your floss colors.

PENS

There are many tools out there to trace your pattern, but I prefer FriXion heat-erasable pens made by Pilot. When you're finished stitching, you can erase any of the excess lines with a hair dryer.

7

Basic Techniques

After you've gathered your materials, it's time to prepare your hoop for stitching!

PREPARE YOUR HOOP

A

B

C

1 Unscrew the metal piece at the top of your outer hoop so you can separate the outer and inner hoops from each other (A).

2 Place a square of your fabric over the inner hoop (the smaller hoop and the hoop without the metal fastening). Then place the outer hoop over both the fabric and the inner hoop (B). Tightly screw the fastening at the top of your hoop.

3 Pull the edges of your fabric all the way around your hoop so the fabric is very taut, like a drum (C). This will not only help during your pattern transfer process but will also help you avoid puckering your fabric during stitching. Trim the edges of your cloth in a circle around your hoop with your fabric scissors. Having clean, crisp edges will make it easier to stitch.

TRANSFERRING YOUR DESIGN

Using a Paper Pattern

Using basic printer paper, you can print out your design to your preferred size. It should be no larger than the size of your hoop. Then, simply place your prepared hoop face down onto the paper. Once you're happy with the placement, use your drawing tool of choice to trace the pattern onto the fabric. This technique works best with lighter colored, transparent fabrics.

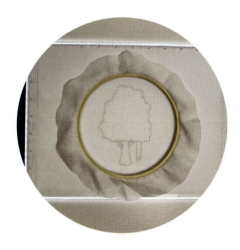

Other Transfer Methods

If you don't like to trace, there are alternative methods to get your pattern of choice onto your fabric. Stick-and-stitch paper (or water-soluble paper) comes in rolls and printer-friendly sheets. This is also the best solution if you're stitching on dark, opaque fabrics. After printing your pattern onto the sheet, peel off the backing before placing the design directly onto your fabric. The pattern is stitched through the paper and the fabric. After you're finished, place the entire project under running water or in a bowl of water until all the paper has dissolved away. Once your project has dried completely, you're all finished!

Using a Light Source

If you have access to a light pad, laptop, tablet, or window, you can use it as a backlight to display your design. Place your printed pattern on top of the pad or light source, then place your prepared hoop face down on top of the paper/pad and start tracing right on the fabric! Again, you'll want to use lightly colored fabrics for this technique.

Using a Digital Pattern

If you don't have a way to print out your pattern, you can trace it digitally! Open your PDF pattern and place your prepared hoop face down on the screen for tracing whether you're using a laptop, tablet, or phone.

With your pattern transferred to your fabric, you're ready to start stitching!

TIP: *After drawing your pattern onto the fabric, as shown in the photos here, separate the hoops and place your design "right side out" before stitching.*

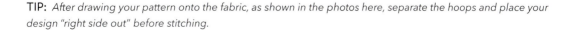

Common Stitches

The patterns in this book use basic, beginner-friendly embroidery stitches. To help make the instructions even simpler, take note of when to push or pull the needle "up" and "down." "Up" means poking the needle through the back of the fabric and pulling up through to the front of the fabric. "Down" means pushing the needle through the front of the fabric and pulling it down through to the back of the fabric.

GETTING STARTED

Splitting Strands

DMC cotton floss, as well as many other flosses, is made up of six individual strands. If a pattern calls for fewer than six strands, you'll need to split the floss apart. Dividing floss can be done a couple of ways: strand by strand or by groups of strands. Pay close attention to how many strands of floss each step of a pattern calls for to have the best finished result.

Threading Your Needle

This is the basic technique for threading one to six strands of floss.

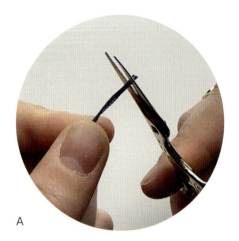

A

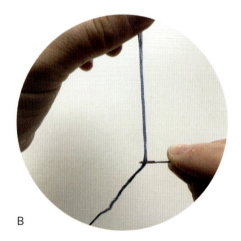

B

1 Cut about a forearm's length of embroidery floss and trim the very end with a pair of sharp scissors. A crisp end will make it easier to thread (A). If necessary, wet the end to keep the strands together.

2 Thread the floss through the eye of the needle and pull through (B). Tie a knot at the long end of the thread.

TIP: If you're using six strands (or fewer), pull the end of the floss through the eye of the needle about a finger's length so it doesn't slip back through the eye while you're stitching.

Threading Twelve Strands

There are times when patterns will call for threading twelve strands of floss to create thick stitchwork. Simply pull the threads all the way through, as you would for six strands, until the ends meet. Tie the two ends together into a knot (C). Now, twelve strands of floss will go through the fabric while stitching.

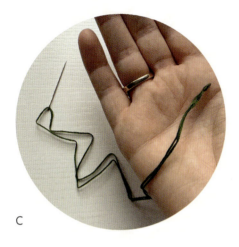

TIP: *When using twelve strands of floss, it's easier to work with a tapestry or chenille needle because they have larger eyes.*

C

FASTENING OFF YOUR FLOSS

When you're almost to the end of your thread during the stitching process, you will want to fasten it to your project before cutting a new strand and continuing.

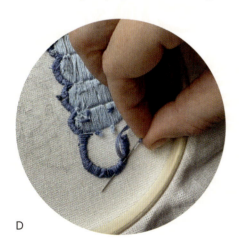

1 Pass the needle down to the back of the work. Weave your needle through the stitches on the back of the work. Crisscross and pass the needle in different directions and through different stitches to secure it in place (D). Trim the excess floss.

D

For video tutorials on common stitches, scan the QR code with your smartphone.

BACKSTITCH

The backstitch is a highly versatile stitch and a perfect one to learn as a complete beginner. This stitch can be used for outlining and lettering.

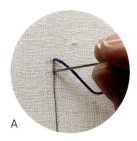

A

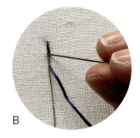

B

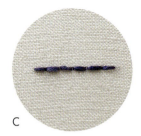

C

1 At the start of the line, go up until the knot stops the floss from going any farther. Go down through the fabric about ¼" (0.5 cm) away from the first stitch (A).

2 Go up through the fabric about ¼" (0.5 cm) away from the previous stitch.

3 Go down, meeting the floss from the previous stitch (B). Continue this way all the way along the line or design section (C). Secure on back when finished.

WHIPPED BACKSTITCH

The whipped backstitch is an extension of the backstitch and creates the look of a smooth line.

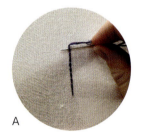

A

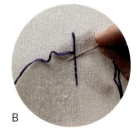

B

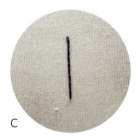

C

1 Follow the instructions for backstitch. With the needle pulled up through the end of the last stitch, weave the needle under the next backstitch from right to left and pull the floss all the way through (A).

2 Weave the needle under the next backstitch, from right to left, and pull through. Continue like this for the entire length (B). Be sure to continue weaving under the backstitches in the same direction, from right to left.

3 End the stitch by taking the needle down at the end of the line (C). Secure on back when finished.

CHAIN STITCH

The chain stitch is great as a filler stitch or to create thick lines.

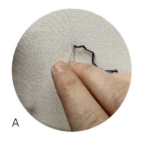
A

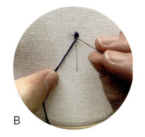
B

C

1 Go up until the knot stops the floss from going any farther. Go down through the hole the needle just created (A), but don't pull all the way through. This creates a loop on the front of the work.

2 Go up, coming through the loop about ¼" (0.5 cm) away from the previous stitch, and pull all the way through (B).

3 To continue the chain, repeat steps 1 and 2. To finish, go down to lock the last loop in place, and finish off the stitch on the back (C).

LAZY DAISY STITCH

Very similar to the chain stitch, the lazy daisy stitch is basically one link of the chain stitch and is great for creating flower petals.

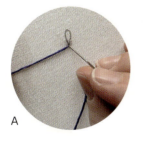
A

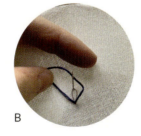
B

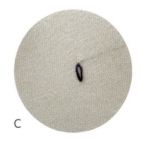
C

1 Go up until the knot stops the floss from going any farther. Go down through the same hole (A), but don't pull all the way through. This creates a loop on the front of the work.

2 Thread the needle back up through the loop (B), and pull tight. Go down just outside the loop to secure it in place.

3 Once secured, this stitch looks like a single flower petal (C). Repeat the previous steps, working in a circle from the center out to create a five-petal daisy. Secure on back when finished.

Common Stitches 13

FRENCH KNOT

French knots create the look of tiny dots and are perfect for adding texture to embroidery. They also enhance flower buds and centers.

A

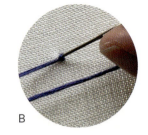

B

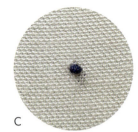

C

1 Go up until the knot stops the floss from going any farther. Hold the floss with one hand and the needle in the other, then wrap the thread around the needle once (A).

2 Hold the floss taut with one hand while the other directs the needle back down, close to the previous hole where the needle first came up (B).

3 Pull all the way through to complete the knot (C). Secure on back when finished.

TIP: *Holding tension on the floss is key to a good French knot. Just be sure not to hold it so tightly that the needle can't go back down through the fabric.*

FISHBONE STITCH

The fishbone stitch is great for making leaves!

A

B

C

1 Start at the point of a leaf shape and make a small straight stitch along the middle line (A).

2 Go up a tiny bit lower than the first stitch on one side.

3 Go down on the middle line slightly lower than the first stitch (B).

4 Repeat steps 2 and 3 on the opposite side of the first stitch. Keep repeating from side to side until the stitches reach the bottom of the leaf (C). Secure on back when finished.

TIP: *Remember, after creating the first stich, your needle needs to just follow the shape of the outer lines and the center line–outside, inside, outside, inside–while alternating sides.*

UNOFFICIAL *Bridgerton* EMBROIDERY

SATIN STITCH

The satin stitch is great for filling in larger areas of a design.

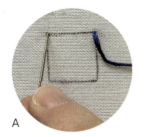

A

B

C

1 Go up until the knot stops the floss from going any farther on one end of the pattern line.

2 Go down on the opposite edge of the pattern line, and pull all the way through (A).

3 Go up again right next to the first stitch, and continue this sequence, filling up the empty space (B, C). Secure on back when finished.

TIP: *Keep the stitches as close together as possible, and make sure the floss doesn't twist between each stitch. Don't be afraid to take stitches out and start again if they start to overlap each other or have too much space between them.*

STRAIGHT STITCH

Straight stitches are clean and simple! They are best used as outlines, but they are also effective as accents to the center of leaves, blending colors, and more. Varying the length to create long and short straight stitches is an interesting effect too.

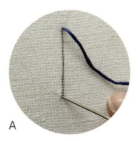
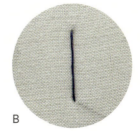

A

B

1 Go up until the knot stops the floss from going any farther.

2 Go down through the fabric to the end of the line following the pattern (A). This completes the straight stitch (B). Secure on back when finished.

Common Stitches   15

WOVEN WHEEL STITCH

The woven wheel stitch looks much more complicated than it actually is! When completed, it creates a roselike look.

A

B

C

1 This stitch can be done with any odd number of starter stitches, but 5 is commonly used. Create 5 straight stitches, making a pinwheel shape along the lines of the pattern, meeting in the middle (A).

2 Come up in between any two of the starter stitches.

3 Start going in one direction in a circle (on top of the fabric) above one starter stitch and below the next (B). Continue like this until the strand of floss is almost to the end.

4 Once the needle can't go under any more of the starter stitches, go down through the fabric and fasten the floss on the back, or add a few extra stitches along the rose to cover up any visible ends of the starter stitches (C). Secure on back when finished.

TIP: Twelve strands will make woven wheel roses look nice and fluffy, while six or fewer strands will make them look a bit smaller and less full.

LOOPS

Loops are great for adding accents to floral patterns, creating thick texture, or even creating leaves. Add them to the inside of woven wheel roses or between elements to fill extra space, such as between flowers of a bouquet.

A

B

1 Go up until the knot stops the floss from going any farther.

2 Carefully go back down close to where the needle came up, but don't pull all the way through, creating a loop (A).

3 Keep doing this to fill the space (B). Secure on back when finished. See Garden Swing Whispers on page 71 for the final loops look.

16 UNOFFICIAL *Bridgerton* EMBROIDERY

Finishing Your Work

There are many ways to finish an embroidery piece once the stitching is completed. Some people like to keep the design inside the working hoop, while others would rather frame it inside a classic photo frame or create an entirely new project out of it. Here is how to finish your work in the hoop.

A

B

C

1 Cut a piece of felt to fit inside the back of the hoop, and let it rest inside the hoop (A).

2 Cut a piece of floss, and knot one end. Thread the floss up through the fabric so the knot is covered by the excess fabric (the knot will be on the inside of the fabric). Weave the needle in and out (this back-and-forth stitch is called a running stitch) through all the excess fabric (B).

3 When you reach the beginning of your hoop, pull the thread tight to gather the fabric (C). Secure the floss in place with a knot, and trim excess thread.

TIP: *The tension of the running stitch through the excess fabric will hold the felt piece in place. This method is a less permanent way of finishing the hoop while making the back look clean.*

Displaying Your Embroideries

You've spent a lot of time and effort stitching your embroidery piece, so you should show it off! If you aren't sure how to display embroidery, here are a few easy ideas. If you've stitched a project as a gift, be sure to share these ideas with the recipient too!

HANGING
Tie a piece of cording, twine, or string to the metal fastening at the top of the hoop, and hang it on the wall. This also works well for creating a gallery wall of hoops!

ART STAND
Use a small art stand, plate stand, or mini easel to rest your finished hoop. A method like this looks great on a bookshelf, and you can easily switch out your hoops throughout the year.

ORNAMENT DISPLAY STAND
Use an ornament display stand so the hoop can both hang and be the center of attention!

Finishing Your Work 17

The Ton's First Stitches

As debutants and bachelors are introduced to society, each hope to take their first steps into the world of dancing, courting, and eventual romance. Think of these projects as your first steps into the world of embroidery! These patterns are beginner friendly, using only a few basic stitches in each. Remember, you can refer to "Common Stitches" (pages 10–16) any time you need a little extra help. After you've stitched a few of these projects, you'll be ready for the projects that are "Fit for the Queen."

Penelope's Blossoms

These citrus colors were inspired by Penelope Featherington. Her sharp wit, strong writing talent, and entrepreneurial spirit are as bright as the warm colors in this piece. This pattern uses a wide array of beginner stitches, perfect for some fundamental practice.

SUPPLIES

6" (15 cm) embroidery hoop
Fabric scissors
Fabric
Embroidery needle
Embroidery scissors

STITCHES

Fishbone Stitch – FS (page 14)
French Knot – FK (page 14)
Satin Stitch – SS (page 15)
Straight Stitch – ST (page 15)
Whipped Backstitch – WBS (page 12)

THREAD

DMC floss colors:
726 – Mimosa
772 – Celery
917 – Dark Magenta
3347 – Asparagus
3689 – Pale Orchid
3823 – Moonshine
3852 – Metallic Glitz
3854 – Chai Spice

NOTE:
This pattern uses all 6 strands of floss.

Penelope's Blossoms template, page 104

1 Prepare the hoop and transfer the pattern. Start with DMC 3852 to create French knots (with a single wrap) in the centers of the large yellow flowers. Complete these flowers with satin stitches for the petals using DMC 726.

2 Use DMC 3823 to create satin stitches for the centers of all the pink flowers. Create the petals of the pink flowers with DMC 3689 and satin stitches. Complete the pink flowers with a straight stitch in each petal center using DMC 917.

3 Use fishbone stitches in DMC 772 to create the leaves for each pink flower. Complete the leaves using a straight stitch down the center in DMC 3689.

4 Use satin stitches in DMC 3347 for the small, rounded leaves for the dark pink and orange flowers (there are four). Complete the dark pink and orange flowers with satin stitches for the petals with DMC 3854 and DMC 917.

5 Use DMC 3347 to create whipped backstitches for the stems coming off the yellow flowers. Using the same green color, create fishbone stitches to create the leaves. Complete the leaves with a straight stitch down each center using DMC 772.

6 Finish this pattern with DMC 3823 using French knots (with a single wrap) for all the small dots scattered throughout the design.

The Ton's First Stitches

A Posy of Violets

This pattern was inspired by the matriarch of the Bridgerton Family, Violet Bridgerton. The little bundle of violets is sweet and simple, a perfect starter pattern to anyone's embroidery journey.

SUPPLIES

6" (15 cm) embroidery hoop
Fabric scissors
Fabric
Embroidery needle
Embroidery scissors

STITCHES

Fishbone Stitch – FS (page 14)
Satin Stitch – SS (page 15)
Whipped Backstitch – WBS (page 12)

THREAD

DMC floss colors:
211 – Pearlescent Light Parma Violet
340 – Wisteria Blue
976 – Nutmeg
3347 – Asparagus
3755 – Pastel Blue

NOTE:
This pattern uses all 6 strands of floss.

A Posy of Violets template, page 106

1 Prepare the hoop and transfer the pattern. Use DMC 976 to create the small orange flower centers using satin stitches.

2 Continuing with satin stitches, use DMC 211 to create the next layer of the flowers surrounding the orange sections. Finish the petals using DMC 340 and satin stitches. This includes the tiny bud on the right side.

3 Create whipped backstitches for the stems using DMC 3347. Continue with DMC 3347 and make fishbone stitches for the leaves.

4 Use a satin stitch in DMC 3347 to create the small segment attached to the bud on the right side. Complete the pattern with a whipped backstitch in DMC 3755 for the bow on the stems.

The Ton's First Stitches

THE Duke's Rose Garden

The front steps of a home are never complete without the inviting blooms of blossoming flowers. This decorative stone pot will provide valuable satin stitch practice, while the woven wheel roses will bring this piece to life.

SUPPLIES

7" (18 cm) embroidery hoop

Fabric scissors

Fabric

Embroidery needle

Embroidery scissors

STITCHES

Fishbone Stitch – FS (page 14)

Satin Stitch – SS (page 15)

Straight Stitch – ST (page 15)

Woven Wheel Stitch – WW (page 16)

THREAD

DMC floss colors:

169 – Tin

3051 – Forest Green

BLANC

NOTE:
This pattern uses all 6 strands of floss unless otherwise noted.

The Duke's Rose Garden template, page 109

1 Prepare the hoop and transfer the pattern. Start with DMC 169 to create satin stitches on all the sections of the planter. Finish the pot with DMC 169 and horizontal straight stitches to divide the sections of the bowl and the base.

2 Use DMC BLANC to create 12-strand woven wheel roses.

3 Create all the stems with straight stitches in DMC 3051, and complete the pattern with fishbone stitch leaves in the same color.

The Ton's First Stitches

Wisteria ON THE Promenade

These beautiful purple blooms are said to signify romance and passionate love. It's only appropriate to stitch such a flower when celebrating the love between the Bridgerton children and their partners. These lovely colors create a whimsical look into the romantic lives of the protagonists.

SUPPLIES

6" (15 cm) embroidery hoop

Fabric scissors

Fabric

Embroidery needle

Embroidery scissors

STITCHES

Fishbone Stitch – FS (page 14)

Satin Stitch – SS (page 15)

Straight Stitch – ST (page 15)

Whipped Backstitch – WBS (page 12)

THREAD

DMC floss colors:

209 – Lilac

211 – Pearlescent Light Parma Violet

471 – Tarragon

552 – Violet

869 – Coffee

NOTE: This pattern uses all 6 strands of floss.

The Ton's First Stitches 33

Wisteria on the Promenade template, page 105

1 Prepare the hoop and transfer the pattern. Start by stitching all the whipped backstitch stems using DMC 471. Then, create fishbone stitch leaves with the same color.

2 Add in the branch using DMC 869 and a satin stitch.

3 Stitch the darkest purple blooms, the ones at the bottoms of the flowers, with DMC 552 using satin stitches worked from the bottom up.

4 Add the second darkest purple, DMC 209, using satin stitches for the six small circles. Complete the purple flowers with DMC 211 and satin stitches.

5 Add in short straight stitches using DMC 471 to connect the darkest purple segments to the rest of the flowers.

The Ton's First Stitches

A Scandalous Quill

This pattern was inspired by Lady Whistledown's ability to chart the course of courtships, scandals, and, of course, the gossip that keeps the ton on its toes. All with the scratch of her quill.

SUPPLIES

6" (15 cm) embroidery hoop

Fabric scissors

Fabric

Embroidery needle

Embroidery scissors

STITCHES

Backstitch – BS (page 12)

Fishbone Stitch – FS (page 14)

French Knot – FK (page 14)

Satin Stitch – SS (page 15)

Whipped Backstitch – WBS (page 12)

THREAD

DMC floss colors:

154 – Prune

522 – Lattice Green

746 – Pearlescent Vanilla

807 – Turquoise Tide

3753 – Moonlight Blue

3808 – Mallard

NOTE:
This pattern uses all 6 strands of floss.

A Scandalous Quill template, page 108

1 Prepare the hoop and transfer the pattern. Start with DMC 3808 to create the bow using satin stitches. Complete the vase with satin stitches in DMC 3753.

2 Continuing with DMC 3753, create single-wrap French knots for all the flower centers. Use DMC 807 and satin stitches to create the next layer of the flowers. Finish the flowers with satin stitch petals in DMC 3808.

3 Use DMC 522 to create whipped backstitches for the stems and fishbone stitches for the leaves.

4 Create satin stitches for the inkwell with DMC 154. Continuing with DMC 154, create backstitches separating each section of satin stitches horizontally.

5 Make the center of the feather with a whipped backstitch in DMC 746 and fishbone stitches for each feather segment.

The Ton's First Stitches

THE *Secret Hive*

A healthy garden is apparent with the presence of bees. Even sweeter? A beehive! This pattern blends a mixture of techniques and stitches that will transform your stitching into a buzzing nature scene.

SUPPLIES

6" (15 cm) embroidery hoop
Fabric scissors
Fabric
Embroidery needle
Embroidery scissors

STITCHES

Backstitch – BS (page 12)
Fishbone Stitch – FS (page 14)
French Knot – FK (page 14)
Running Stitch – RS (page 17)
Satin Stitch – SS (page 15)
Whipped Backstitch – WBS (page 12)

THREAD

DMC floss colors:
310 – Metallic Black
729 – Honey
743 – Banana
839 – Root Brown
3346 – Artichoke
3726 – Iced Plum
Diamant D140

NOTE: This pattern uses all 6 strands of floss.

The Ton's First Stitches

The Secret Hive template, page 105

1 Prepare the hoop and transfer the pattern. Use DMC 839 to create satin stitch branches.

2 With DMC 743, create French knots in the flower centers, wrapping the needle just once. Complete the flowers with satin stitch petals in DMC 3726.

3 Use DMC 3346 to create fishbone stitch leaves and backstitch stems.

4 To create the beehive, use DMC 839 and a satin stitch as the hive opening and DMC 729 and satin stitches for the remaining segments.

5 All three bees are created the same way: Start with the satin stitch bodies, alternating colors DMC 310 and DMC 743. Create the wings in Diamant D140 with whipped backstitches.

6 The bee paths use DMC 310 and a running stitch. A running stitch is similar to a straight stitch. Refer to the Finishing Your Work section on page 17 to learn about running stitches.

The Ton's First Stitches

Featherington's Flowers

The road to marriage was rocky for Penelope and Colin, but in the end, they flourished with a foundation of friendship. The yellow roses in this bouquet symbolize just that, surrounded by the beautiful Bridgerton blue hues. Let's raise a glass, or an embroidery needle, to their partnership!

SUPPLIES

6" (15 cm) embroidery hoop
Fabric scissors
Fabric
Embroidery needle
Embroidery scissors

STITCHES

Backstitch – BS (page 12)
Fishbone Stitch – FS (page 14)
French Knot – FK (page 14)
Satin Stitch – SS (page 15)
Woven Wheel Stitch – WW (page 16)

THREAD

DMC floss colors:
341 – Hydrangea Blue
523 – Green Ash
931 – Blue Grey
932 – Blue Gull
3823 – Moonshine
3840 – Linen Flower Blue
BLANC

NOTE:
This pattern uses all 6 strands of floss unless otherwise noted.

The Ton's First Stitches 45

Featherington's Flowers template, page 108

1 Prepare the hoop and transfer the pattern. Start with DMC 3823 to create 12-strand woven wheel roses.

2 Create satin stitches in DMC 931 and DMC 341 for all the petaled flowers.

3 Use DMC 523 to create backstitches for the stems and fishbone stitches for the leaves.

4 Create the hyacinths using DMC 3840 and French knots, wrapping the needle just once. Fill in the rest of the bouquet's center using additional single-wrap French knots in DMC BLANC.

5 Use DMC 932 and a satin stitch to create the ribbon sections.

The Ton's First Stitches

THE Gentleman's Balloon

Colin Bridgerton valiantly saves Penelope Featherington from a rogue hot-air balloon in a fan-favorite scene. This piece was inspired by Colin's heroic deed, as it brought the pair that much closer together.

SUPPLIES

6" (15 cm) embroidery hoop

Fabric scissors

Fabric

Embroidery needle

Embroidery scissors

STITCHES

Backstitch – BS (page 12)

Fishbone Stitch – FS (page 14)

Satin Stitch – SS (page 15)

Straight Stitch – ST (page 15)

Whipped Backstitch – WBS (page 12)

THREAD

DMC floss colors:

30 – Kitten Gray

435 – Tobacco

797 – French Blue

819 – Layette

3813 – Lichen Green

3822 – Corn Husk

Diamant D3821

NOTE:
This pattern uses all 6 strands of floss.

The Ton's First Stitches

The Gentleman's Balloon template, page 107

1 Prepare the hoop and transfer the pattern. In DMC 797, create lines of whipped backstitch on the top and bottom of the center band of the balloon. Fill the balloon's segments with satin stitches in DMC 3822 and DMC 797.

2 Use DMC 3822 and whipped backstitch to create the circles in the center band of the balloon. Then use DMC 797 to fill in the center band with satin stitches.

3 Continuing with DMC 797, create backstitches between all the alternating segments of the balloon.

4 Use DMC 435 and satin stitches to fill the basket. Then divide each segment with straight stitches in the same color. Work whipped backstitches with DMC 435 to add in the ropes.

5 Use satin stitches to create the flowers with DMC 819 for the centers and DMC 30 for the petals. Complete the flowers with straight stitches in DMC 819 in the centers of the petals.

6 Use DMC 3813 and fishbone stitches to create the leaves. Then finish with Diamant D3821 and straight stitches to create gold accents for the lines in the circles of the middle band and the centers of the leaves.

The Ton's First Stitches   51

Music in the Drawing Room

It's only appropriate that a musical family like the Bridgertons should have a pianoforte to grace one of their rooms. This pattern was inspired by the floral accents inside the Bridgerton home paired with their main source of musical recreation.

SUPPLIES

6" (15 cm) embroidery hoop
Fabric scissors
Fabric
Embroidery needle
Embroidery scissors

STITCHES

Fishbone Stitch – FS (page 14)
French Knot – FK (page 14)
Lazy Daisy Stitch – LD (page 13)
Satin Stitch – SS (page 15)
Straight Stitch – ST (page 15)

THREAD

DMC floss colors:

33 – Allium
157 – Heliotrope
310 – Metallic Black
400 – Conker
797 – French Blue
832 – Modoré
3051 – Forest Green
3823 – Moonshine

NOTE:
This pattern uses all 6 strands of floss.

The Ton's First Stitches

Music in the Drawing Room template, page 108

1 Prepare the hoop and transfer the pattern. Create the body of the piano and the base of the keys in DMC 400 using satin stitches. Create the rectangular box (on the thicker section of the body) and the dividing line between the keys and the body using straight stitches.

2 Create the piano legs and lid using a whipped backstitch in DMC 400. Stitch a piano key with a satin stitch using DMC 310.

3 Use DMC 832 to create the gold accent on the front leg and wheels of the piano using satin stitches. Create the music stand with DMC 400 and straight stitches.

4 Use French knots, wrapping the needle once, with DMC 157 to create the hyacinths. Use DMC 33 to create lazy daisy stitch petals for the pink flowers. For the striped flowers, create satin stitches in DMC 3823 for the centers and straight stitch petals in DMC 797 and DMC 157.

5 Complete the pattern using DMC 3051 to create fishbone stitch leaves and straight stitch stems.

The Ton's First Stitches

A Cake Fit for a Duchess

Let them eat cake! Oh, wait, wrong storyline. Plenty of extravagant weddings take place in the **Bridgerton** *universe, which calls for some delicious stitching. The adornment of sugary flowers makes this cake good enough for a duke and duchess.*

SUPPLIES

5" (13 cm) embroidery hoop
Fabric scissors
Fabric
Embroidery needle
Embroidery scissors

STITCHES

Backstitch – BS (page 12)
Fishbone Stitch – FS (page 14)
French Knot – FK (page 14)
Satin Stitch – SS (page 15)
Straight Stitch – ST (page 15)
Whipped Backstitch – WBS (page 12)

THREAD

DMC floss colors:
30 – Kitten Gray
157 – Heliotrope
924 – Tahitian Pearl
3727 – Lycee
3747 – Pearlescent Ice Blue
3803 – Bordeaux
BLANC

NOTE:
This pattern uses all 6 strands of floss.

A Cake Fit for a Dutchess template, page 102

1 Prepare the hoop and transfer the pattern. Starting with the largest flower and using DMC 3727, stitch French knots in the flower centers, wrapping the needle once. Then add the satin stitch petals with DMC 30.

2 Next, add fishbone stitch leaves coming out of the purple flower in DMC 924. Add the straight stitch stems in the same color. For the stems extending through the center of the cake, use large backstitches or a whipped backstitch.

3 Complete the floral sprigs off the purple flower with satin stitch buds in DMC 157 and 2 single-wrap French knots on the left side in DMC 30.

4 Using DMC 3727, create another single-wrap French knot in the center of the cake. Add satin stitches extending from the French knot using DMC 3803 and DMC 3727. Stitch 3 tidy rows of French knots in DMC BLANC.

5 At the top of the cake, add in the single-wrap French knots in DMC 3727. Add the petals of the flower in DMC 157 using satin stitches. Complete the top flower with fishbone stitch leaves and straight stitch stems in DMC 924 and French knot buds in DMC 30.

6 Fill the layers of cake using satin stitches in DMC 3747.

The Ton's First Stitches

Fit for the Queen

Her majesty expects nothing but the best from her subjects. With the patterns in this chapter, you'll shine as bright as her diamonds as you tackle projects that are a bit more challenging. The extra time and attention to detail will be well worth the effort.

Unwed Monogram

Monogram etiquette suggests that until you're married, just a single letter should be used for your monogram. When married, your monogram may have two or three letters. Here, B, of course, stands for the many unwed Bridgerton children. Their classiness and elegance inspired the flourishes that surround the bold blue letter.

SUPPLIES

6" (15 cm) embroidery hoop
Fabric scissors
Fabric
Embroidery needle
Embroidery scissors

STITCHES

Fishbone Stitch – FS (page 14)
French Knot – FK (page 14)
Satin Stitch – SS (page 15)

THREAD

DMC floss colors:
336 – Indigo Blue
930 – Slate Grey
932 – Blue Gull
3042 – Storm Clouds
3072 – Thunderous Skies
3753 – Moonlight Blue

> **NOTE:**
> This pattern uses all 6 strands of floss.

Fit for the Queen

Unwed Monogram template, page 106

1 Prepare the hoop and transfer the pattern. Stitch the *B* with DMC 336 and satin stitches.

2 Use fishbone stitches to create leaves in DMC 3072, DMC 3042, and DMC 932.

3 Create satin stitches with DMC 3753 for the rounded elements.

4 Complete the pattern by creating the small blue flowers: Make a French knot with a single wrap in the centers using DMC 3072, then satin stitch with DMC 930 and DMC 932.

Fit for the Queen

THE *Residence*

Who wouldn't want to live in the elegant home of the Bridgerton family? This technical piece is great practice for the chain stitch and French knots. Get ready to create an abundance of wisteria and vines growing on the brick facade.

SUPPLIES

7" (18 cm) embroidery hoop
Fabric scissors
Fabric
Embroidery needle
Embroidery scissors

STITCHES

Chain Stitch – CS (page 13)
French Knot – FK (page 14)
Satin Stitch – SS (page 15)
Straight Stitch – ST (page 15)
Whipped Backstitch – WBS (page 12)

THREAD

DMC floss colors:

210 – Parma Violet
225 – Cherry Blossom
400 – Conker
452 – Pigeon Gray
3053 – Avocado
3345 – Spinach
3346 – Artichoke
3865 – Edelweiss

NOTE:
This pattern uses all 6 strands of floss unless otherwise noted.

The Residence template, page 106

1 Prepare the hoop and transfer the pattern. With DMC 400, work chain stitch on the body of the house to give the look of brick.

2 Use DMC 3345 to create French knots, wrapping the needle once, for vines on the upper part of the house. Use DMC 210 to create single-wrap French knots of purple wisteria flowers that divide the two levels of the house.

3 Create the bushes on the ground level using French knots in DMC 3346 and DMC 225, wrapping the needle once.

4 Create the two small flowering trees on either end of the ground level using single-wrap French knots in DMC 3053 and DMC 3865. Finally, add single-wrap French knots underneath the windows of the upper level in DMC 3053.

5 Add satin stitches in DMC 3865 for the windowsills of the three middle windows of the upper level. Continue with DMC 3865 to create windowpanes using straight stitches with 3 strands.

6 Use DMC 452 to create whipped backstitches for the horizontal lines of the railing on top of the house. Fill in the vertical lines using straight stitches in the same color. Complete the two blocks on top of the house in DMC 400 with satin stitches for the rectangles and small straight stitches pointing upward to finish.

Fit for the Queen

Garden Swing Whispers

The tree swing in the garden on the grounds of the Bridgerton house is Eloise's favorite spot to daydream. It's also the spot where many of the Bridgerton siblings converge to exchange whispers about life events. Stitch your own garden swing with a mighty tree full of spring blooms.

SUPPLIES

6" (15 cm) embroidery hoop
Fabric scissors
Fabric
Embroidery needle
Embroidery scissors

STITCHES

Loops – L (page 16)
Satin Stitch – SS (page 15)
Whipped Backstitch – WBS (page 12)

THREAD

DMC floss colors:

420 – Hazelnut
646 – Smoke Grey
904 – Kale
3713 – Rose Quartz

NOTE:
This pattern uses all 6 strands of floss unless otherwise noted.

Fit for the Queen

Garden Swing Whispers template, page 109

1 Prepare the hoop and transfer the pattern. Create 12-strand loops using DMC 904 and DMC 3713, filling the foliage of the tree. Change the direction of the loops to create the look of a healthy, flourishing tree. Tip: Start with all the DMC 904 loops where desired and then go back with DMC 3713 to fill in the gaps, creating flowers.

2 Use DMC 420 to satin stitch the trunk and the seat swing.

3 Use DMC 646 to work whipped backstitch for the swing's ropes.

Fit for the Queen

Danbury's Diadem

Lady Danbury's sharp wit is equal to that of her striking wardrobe. This piece was inspired by one of her many glittering crowns, which will be brought to life using metallic thread. Though more technical and detailed, this pattern will be one to treasure once completed.

SUPPLIES

6" (15 cm) embroidery hoop

Fabric scissors

Fabric

Embroidery needle

Embroidery scissors

STITCHES

Backstitch – BS (page 12)

Fishbone Stitch – FS (page 14)

French Knot – FK (page 14)

Lazy Daisy Stitch – LD (page 13)

Satin Stitch – SS (page 15)

Straight Stitch – ST (page 15)

Whipped Backstitch – WBS (page 12)

THREAD

DMC floss colors:

168 – Metallic Town Mouse Grey

311 – Dark Polar Blue

Diamant D168

NOTE: This pattern uses all 6 strands of floss unless otherwise noted.

Fit for the Queen

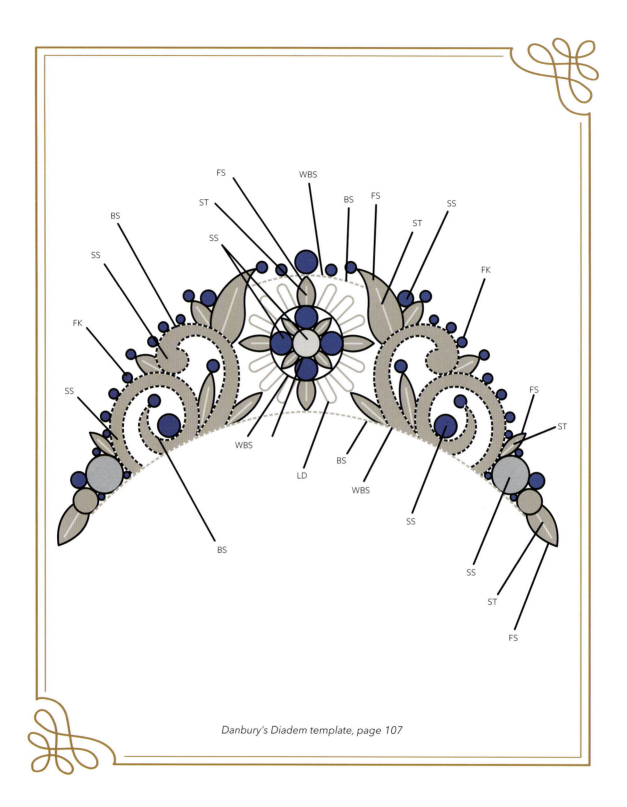

Danbury's Diadem template, page 107

1 Prepare the hoop and transfer the pattern. With 3 strands of DMC 168, work whipped backstitch on the upper and lower arches of the crown and the two thin circles in the center. Continue with DMC 168 and satin stitches to fill the large, curved elements and larger circles on either side of the base.

2 Fill in all the leaves with fishbone stitches using 3 strands of DMC 168.

3 Use 3 strands of DMC 311 to stitch the remaining circles using satin stitch for larger circles and single-wrap French knots for the small accent circles.

4 Using Diamant D168, create lazy daisy stitches for the silver accents in the crown center. Continuing with Diamant D168, fill the center gem and two large circles with satin stitch.

5 Backstitch with Diamant D168 along the upper and lower arches and surrounding the curved elements. Complete the pattern with straight stitches inside all the leaves using Diamant D168.

Fit for the Queen

Tea with the Ton

It's teatime, and who wouldn't want at least one cup of this delightfully brewed beverage while stitching an elegant teapot? Perhaps what is so intriguing about tea sets is the vast variety of patterns, colors, shapes, and sizes they come in. Inspired by England's most famous beverage, this teapot design combines the beauty of English gardens with a "cuppa."

SUPPLIES

5" (15 cm) embroidery hoop
Fabric scissors
Fabric
Embroidery needle
Embroidery scissors

STITCHES

Backstitch – BS (page 12)
Fishbone Stitch – FS (page 14)
French Knot – FK (page 14)
Satin Stitch – SS (page 15)
Straight Stitch – ST (page 15)
Whipped Backstitch – WBS (page 12)

THREAD

DMC floss colors:
25 – Cornflower White
33 – Allium
522 – Lattice Green
3042 – Storm Clouds
3836 – Thyme Flower
Diamant D168

NOTE:
This pattern uses all 6 strands of floss.

Fit for the Queen

Tea with the Ton template, page 103

1 Prepare the hoop and transfer the pattern. The upper and lower body of the teapot, the base, the rim, and the tip of the lid are all made with satin stitches. The lighter purple segments use DMC 25, while the darker purple uses DMC 3042.

2 Use Diamant D168 to create straight stitches down the main sections of the upper body of the teapot.

3 Using DMC 3836, add 4 French knots in the middle of the teapot, wrapping the needle once. Stitch single-wrap French knots with DMC 3836 and DMC 33 for the lilac.

4 Using DMC 3042, work a whipped backstitch outline on the handle. Add in satin stitches to fill the empty space of the handle with DMC 25.

5 Use whipped backstitch for the stem of the lilac with DMC 522.

6 Use a fishbone stitch to embroider the leaf in DMC 522. Add in back-stitches with Diamant D169 along the center line of the leaf.

Fit for the Queen 81

THE *Regency Teacup*

Bursting with soft-colored blooms, this teacup is ready to dress up any tea table for a beautiful gathering. This tea party–inspired pattern is a great project to take on to practice the satin stitch. Cheers to cool colors and hot tea!

SUPPLIES

6" (15 cm) embroidery hoop
Fabric scissors
Fabric
Embroidery needle
Embroidery scissors

STITCHES

Fishbone Stitch – FS (page 14)
French Knot – FK (page 14)
Satin Stitch – SS (page 15)
Straight Stitch – ST (page 15)
Whipped Backstitch – WBS (page 12)

THREAD

DMC floss colors:

211 – Pearlescent Light Parma Violet
322 – Delft Blue
340 – Wisteria Blue
800 – Sky Blue
924 – Tahitian Pearl
926 – Grey Green
3013 – Green Oyster
3051 – Forest Green
3865 – Edelweiss

NOTE:
This pattern uses all 6 strands of floss.

The Regency Teacup template, page 103

1 Prepare the hoop and transfer the pattern. Satin stitch the body of the teacup with DMC 800, filling the largest sections first. Add satin stitches on the rim, base, and handle using DMC 322.

2 Complete the saucer from top to bottom (rim, plate body, and base) with satin stitches using the same colors, DMC 800 and DMC 322.

3 Create single-wrap French knots with DMC 3865 in the flower centers. For the purple flowers, add satin stitch petals with DMC 340 and then DMC 211. Work from the center outward.

4 For the main blue flower, add satin stitch petals with DMC 924 and then DMC 926. Again, work from the center outward. The other teal flower petals bordering the rim of the teacup just need satin stitches in DMC 926.

5 Fishbone stitch with DMC 3051 for the large leaves and DMC 3013 for the smaller leaves. DMC 3013 is also used to create whipped backstitch stems for the smaller leaves. Use the same colors to create a straight stitch down the center of each finished leaf in the opposite color.

6 Complete the pattern with single-wrap French knots using DMC 3865 for the remaining white space in between the larger flowers.

Fit for the Queen

Mystery of the Masquerade

Add some mystery and intrigue to the next ball of the season with a gilded mask. No one will recognize the wearer with the intricate satin stitches and French knots this pattern holds. Enjoy adding in the gold accents at the end to tie this piece together!

SUPPLIES

6" (15 cm) embroidery hoop

Fabric scissors

Fabric

Embroidery needle

Embroidery scissors

STITCHES

Backstitch – BS (page 12)

Fishbone Stitch – FS (page 14)

French Knot – FK (page 14)

Satin Stitch – SS (page 15)

Straight Stitch – ST (page 15)

Whipped Backstitch – WBS (page 12)

THREAD

DMC floss colors:

29 – Emperor Purple

223 – Granite Pink

814 – Vin Rouge

924 – Tahitian Pearl

3041 – Purple Slate

3042 – Storm Clouds

3713 – Rose Quartz

B5200 – Pearlescent White Light

Diamant D3821

> **NOTE:**
> This pattern uses all 6 strands of floss.

Fit for the Queen

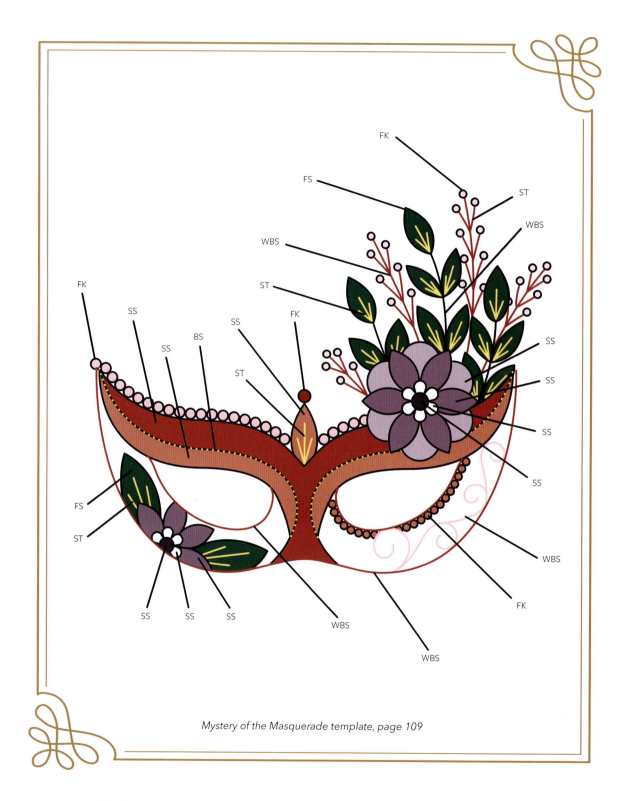

Mystery of the Masquerade template, page 109

1. Prepare the hoop and transfer the pattern. Fill the main section of the mask with satin stitch using DMC 814. Continue with the satin stitch for the next layer using DMC 223. Include the triangular section in the middle at the top.

2. Use DMC 814 and whipped backstitches for the eye hole outline and the remaining outline of the mask.

3. Use DMC 29 to satin stitch the flowers. Continue working on these flowers and satin stitches using DMC B5200 for the middle layer and DMC 3041 for the pointed petals. The large flower has an additional section of satin stitch petals in DMC 3042.

4. Use DMC 924 to create whipped backstitches for the stems on the top of the mask.

5. Continue with DMC 924 to work fishbone stitches for the leaves on the bottom left and the top of the mask. Use DMC 223 to create whipped backstitch stems extending from the top of the mask and straight stitches for the tiny branches. Use DMC 3713 to create single-wrap French knots on the ends of the tiny branches and along the top border of the mask. Continue with DMC 3713 and make whipped backstitch swirls on the bottom right of the mask.

6. Complete the bottom right of the mask with single-wrap French knots in DMC 223. The last French knot will be in DMC 814 at the tip of the triangular section in the middle. Use Diamant D3821 to add gold accents. Create backstitches separating the red and pink sections of the mask, and add straight stitches to all the leaf centers and the triangular section at the top.

Fit for the Queen   89

Butterflies AND Bubbly

The Featherington family can really put on a party to remember! Their clever use of butterflies made their ball one everyone will talk about for seasons to come. Pair with a glass of satin stitch champagne, and this pattern is ready to clink glasses.

SUPPLIES

6" (15 cm) embroidery hoop
Fabric scissors
Fabric
Embroidery needle
Embroidery scissors

STITCHES

Backstitch – BS (page 12)
French Knot – FK (page 14)
Satin Stitch – SS (page 15)
Straight Stitch – ST (page 15)
Whipped Backstitch – WBS (page 12)

THREAD

DMC floss colors:

310 – Metallic Black
746 – Pearlescent Vanilla
3820 – Sunshine
3827 – Coral Blush
BLANC
Diamant D3821

> **NOTE:**
> This pattern uses all 6 strands of floss unless otherwise noted.

Fit for the Queen

Butterflies and Bubbly template, page 107

1 Prepare the hoop and transfer the pattern. Using DMC 3820, backstitch the outline of the glass. Use Diamant D3821 to weave through the backstitches, creating a dual-colored whipped backstitch.

2 Use DMC 3820 to fill the glass stem with satin stitches. Fill in the glass with DMC 746 and a satin stitch. Use DMC BLANC to stitch a French knot, wrapping the needle once for each bubble.

3 With 3 strands of DMC 310, satin stitch the black areas of the butterflies. Complete the wings with satin stitches in 3 strands of DMC 3827.

4 Use Diamant D3821 again to create straight stitches for the antennae and in between the decorative stem sections of the glass.

Fit for the Queen

THE *Blooming Bee*

The Bridgerton patriarch lost his life to a bee sting, and the family was forever changed. The elegance of the Regency era inspired this piece by using symmetry to combine the bee and the floral motifs. Stitch a special remembrance, as Victorians were known to do, when making this challenging design.

SUPPLIES

6" (15 cm) embroidery hoop
Fabric scissors
Fabric
Embroidery needle
Embroidery scissors

STITCHES

Backstitch – BS (page 12)
Fishbone Stitch – FS (page 14)
French Knot – FK (page 14)
Satin Stitch – SS (page 15)
Straight Stitch – ST (page 15)
Whipped Backstitch – WBS (page 12)
Woven Wheel Stitch – WW (page 16)

THREAD

DMC floss colors:
310 – Metallic Black
730 – Khaki
743 – Banana
830 – Cork Oak
926 – Grey Green
950 – Beige
Diamant D140

NOTE:
This pattern uses all 6 strands of floss unless otherwise noted.

Fit for the Queen

The Blooming Bee template, page 105

1 Prepare the hoop and transfer the pattern. Stitch the bee using DMC 310 and a satin stitch to create the head, thorax, and abdomen. Alternate the body segments with satin stitches in DMC 743.

2 Use 3 strands of DMC 310 to embroider straight stitches for the front legs and backstitches for the back legs. Finish the bee with Diamant D140 floss and whipped backstitch for the wings and antennae.

3 Using DMC 730, create the diamond-shaped curved lines with backstitch. Add fishbone stitch in DMC 730 to the small leaves. Use straight stitch in the same color at each point of the diamond to create flower stems. Add straight stitches down the center of each leaf using Diamant D140.

4 Use DMC 950 and 12 strands of floss to create single-wrap French knot clusters for the flowers at each point of the diamond. Use the same technique and color for centers of the four roses.

5 Work woven wheel stitch for the four roses using 12 strands of floss and DMC 926. Complete the four roses with fishbone stitch leaves using DMC 830. Embellish the center of each leaf with a straight stitch in Diamant D140.

Fit for the Queen   97

YOUR *Carriage Awaits*

The only way to arrive at the next debutant ball is in the glittering structure of a beautiful horse-drawn carriage. Queen Charlotte inspired this piece with the royal purple hues and sparkling gold accents. Once completed, this hoop is fit for a queen!

SUPPLIES

5" (13 cm) embroidery hoop
Fabric scissors
Fabric
Embroidery needle
Embroidery scissors

STITCHES

Backstitch – BS (page 12)
French Knot – FK (page 14)
Satin Stitch – SS (page 15)
Straight Stitch – ST (page 15)
Whipped Backstitch – WBS (page 12)

THREAD

DMC floss colors:
04 – Shadow
154 – Prune
3042 – Storm Clouds
3836 – Thyme Flower
3866 – Garlic White
Diamant D3821

NOTE:
This pattern uses all 6 strands of floss.

Fit for the Queen

Your Carriage Awaits template, page 102

1 Prepare the hoop and transfer the pattern. Satin stitch sections of the carriage using the following colors before adding the gold accents: main body of the carriage, teardrop shape on arch, and seat in DMC 154; top arch in DMC 3042; curtains in DMC 3836; horizontal top of door and wheels in DMC 04; and carriage base in DMC 3866.

2 Once all the main satin stitch areas are complete, use DMC 154 and Diamant D3821 to work whipped backstitch down the center of the carriage and the swirls on the doors. To get the candy cane–striped effect, use DMC 154 first for the backstitch and Diamant D3821 to weave through the backstitch.

3 Finish the door of the carriage with satin stitches in DMC 3042. Create a final straight stitch line down the center of the door with Diamant D3821.

4 Embellish the curtains with small single-wrap French knots along the border in DMC 3866. Complete the wheels with French knots in the centers and straight stitches for the spokes in DMC 04.

5 Add the footstep using straight stitch in DMC 154 and fill the rectangle with a satin stitch in DMC 3836.

6 To create the swirls in the front and back of the carriage, use a whipped backstitch with DMC 3866 and Diamant D3821. Create the whipped backstitches in DMC 3866 first, and then use Diamant D3821. Backstitch the swirls on top of the carriage and behind the seat using Diamant D3821.

7 To complete the section under the seat, create a satin stitch in DMC 3042 (separating the cream-colored swirls and the seat) and a straight stitch using Diamant D3821. The two gold segments separating the top of the carriage and the arch are satin stitches in Diamant D3821.

8 The final gold segments are backstitches that border the arch on the top and the bottom of the cream-colored base. Both use Diamant D3821. The remaining French knots are done in DMC 3836.

Fit for the Queen

Templates

The templates shown here have been sized to easily fit a 4" (10 cm) hoop. Use the QR code provided or visit https://www.quarto.com/files/UnofficialBridgertonEmbroidery to download and print templates at the full size shown in each tutorial. You can scale the printable templates to suit your needs.

Templates 105

Templates 107

Templates 109

About the Author

After the world shut down in 2020 due to the COVID-19 pandemic and I lost my job, I found myself with an abundance of free time to explore the art of embroidery. I had some supplies that I picked up from a yard sale on a whim and took a deep dive into YouTube to learn some techniques.

Drawing has been my primary form of artistic self-expression during my life, but I quickly realized that my own designs would translate well to embroidery patterns. All the designs you will find in this book have been drawn by hand. It's incredibly satisfying to see the line art come to life through embroidery floss as you add each stitch type!

Perhaps like many of you who have picked up this book, you watched *Bridgerton* when it first aired during lockdown (or read the books!). All the beautiful florals, whimsical colors, and English accents served as a perfect form of escapism for me and inspired the designs you'll find amongst these pages.

This book is intended for anyone who would like to learn hand embroidery or for those who are Regency-era enthusiasts who want to create some new patterns. Whatever your reason, thank you for selecting my work, and I hope you feel more empowered to continue your embroidery journey with confidence and joy!

For my parents, whose unwavering encouragement to explore the arts made me into the person I am today; for Greg, for always supporting my artistic goals; and for Isla, for changing my world right alongside the making of this book.

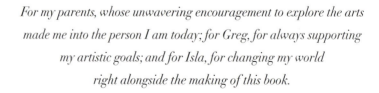

Index

B
Backstitch, about, 12
The Blooming Bee, 94-97, 105
Butterflies and Bubbly, 90-93, 107

C
A Cake Fit for a Duchess, 56-59, 102
Chain stitch, about, 13

D
Danbury's Diadem, 74-77, 107
Designs, transferring, 8-9
Displaying embroidery, 17
The Duke's Rose Garden, 28-31, 109

E
Embroidery floss
  about, 7
  fastening, 10-11
  splitting, 10

F
Fabric, about, 7
Featherington's Flowers, 44-47, 108
Finishing, 17
Fishbone stitch, about, 14
French knot, about, 14

G
Garden Swing Whispers, 70-73, 109
The Gentleman's Balloon, 48-51, 107

H
Hoops
  about, 7
  preparing, 8

L
Lazy daisy stitch, about, 13
Loops, about, 16

M
Music in the Drawing Room, 52-55, 108
Mystery of the Masquerade, 86-89, 109

N
Needles
  about, 7
  threading, 10-11

P
Patterns
  The Blooming Bee, 94-97, 105
  Butterflies and Bubbly, 90-93, 107
  A Cake Fit for a Duchess, 56-59, 102
  Danbury's Diadem, 74-77, 107
  The Duke's Rose Garden, 28-31, 109
  Featherington's Flowers, 44-47, 108
  Garden Swing Whispers, 70-73, 109
  The Gentleman's Balloon, 48-51, 107
  Music in the Drawing Room, 52-55, 108
  Mystery of the Masquerade, 86-89, 109
  Penelope's Blossoms, 20-23, 104
  A Posy of Violets, 24-27, 106
  The Regency Teacup, 82-85, 103
  The Residence, 66-69, 106
  A Scandalous Quilt, 36-39, 108
  The Secret Hive, 40-43, 105
  Tea with the Ton, 78-81, 103
  Unwed Monogram, 62-65, 106
  Wisteria on the Promenade, 32-35, 105
  Your Carriage Awaits, 98-101, 102
Penelope's Blossoms, 20-23, 104
Pens, about, 7
A Posy of Violets, 24-27, 106

R
The Regency Teacup, 82-85, 103
The Residence, 66-69, 106

S
Satin stitch, about, 15
A Scandalous Quilt, 36-39, 108
Scissors, about, 7
The Secret Hive, 40-43, 105

Stitches
  starting, 10-11
  types of
    backstitch, 12
    chain, 13
    fishbone, 14
    French knot, 14
    lazy daisy, 13
    loops, 16
    satin, 15
    straight, 15
    whipped backstitch, 12
    woven wheel, 15
Straight stitch, about, 15

T
Tea with the Ton, 78-81, 103
Templates
  The Blooming Bee, 105
  Butterflies and Bubbly, 107
  A Cake Fit for a Duchess, 102
  Danbury's Diadem, 107
  The Duke's Rose Garden, 109
  Featherington's Flowers, 108
  Garden Swing Whispers, 109
  The Gentleman's Balloon, 107
  Music in the Drawing Room, 108
  Mystery of the Masquerade, 109
  Penelope's Blossoms, 104
  A Posy of Violets, 106
  The Regency Teacup, 103
  The Residence, 106
  A Scandalous Quilt, 108
  The Secret Hive, 105
  Tea with the Ton, 103
  Unwed Monogram, 106
  Wisteria on the Promenade, 105
  Your Carriage Awaits, 102

U
Unwed Monogram, 62-65, 106

W
Whipped backstitch, about, 12
Wisteria on the Promenade, 32-35, 105
Woven wheel stitch, about, 15

Y
Your Carriage Awaits, 98-101, 102

ACKNOWLEDGMENTS

The opportunity to author a book would not have been possible without my editor, Kerry Bogert. I cannot thank you enough for taking a chance on me and leading me through this exciting process.

Brian, thank you for all your support and patience throughout the years and for believing in my work.

Quarto.com

© 2025 Quarto Publishing Group USA Inc.
Text, Photos, Illustrations © 2025 Hilary Dorr

First published in 2025 by Quarry Books, an imprint of The Quarto Group, 100 Cummings Center, Suite 265-D, Beverly, MA 01915, USA.
T (978) 282-9590 F (978) 283-2742

All rights reserved. No part of this book may be reproduced in any form without written permission of the copyright owners. All images in this book have been reproduced with the knowledge and prior consent of the artists concerned, and no responsibility is accepted by producer, publisher, or printer for any infringement of copyright or otherwise, arising from the contents of this publication. Every effort has been made to ensure that credits accurately comply with information supplied. We apologize for any inaccuracies that may have occurred and will resolve inaccurate or missing information in a subsequent reprinting of the book.

Quarry Books titles are also available at discount for retail, wholesale, promotional, and bulk purchase. For details, contact the Special Sales Manager by email at specialsales@quarto.com or by mail at The Quarto Group, Attn: Special Sales Manager, 100 Cummings Center, Suite 265-D, Beverly, MA 01915, USA.

10 9 8 7 6 5 4 3 2 1

ISBN: 978-0-7603-9692-6

Digital edition published in 2025
eISBN: 978-0-7603-9693-3

Library of Congress Cataloging-in-Publication Data available

Design: Ashlee Wadeson Design
Page Layout: Brenda C. Canales
Illustrations: Sue A. Friend

Printed in China